FLORIDA

A PICTORIAL SOUVENIR

CAROL M. HIGHSMITH AND TED LANDPHAIR

FLORIDA

A PICTORIAL SOUVENIR

CRESCENT BOOKS

NEW YORK

THE AUTHORS GRATEFULLY ACKNOWLEDGE
THE SUPPORT PROVIDED BY
HILTON HOTELS CORPORATION
AND
THE KEY WEST HILTON RESORT AND MARINA
THE MIAMI AIRPORT HILTON AND TOWERS
THE PALM BEACH AIRPORT HILTON
THE SAINT PETERSBURG BAYFRONT HILTON
IN CONNECTION WITH THE COMPLETION OF THIS BOOK

————

This 1998 edition is published by Crescent Books®,
a division of Random House Value Publishing, Inc.,
201 East 50th Street, New York, N.Y. 10022.

Crescent Books® and colophon are registered trademarks of
Random House Value Publishing, Inc.

Random House
New York • Toronto • London • Sydney • Auckland
http://www.randomhouse.com/

Printed and bound in China

Library of Congress Cataloging-in-Publication Data
Highsmith, Carol M., 1946–
Florida / Carol M. Highsmith and Ted Landphair.
p.   cm. — (A pictorial souvenir)
ISBN 0-517-20182-8
1. Florida—Tours. 2. Florida—Pictorial works.
3. Florida—Description and travel.
I. Landphair, Ted, 1942–   . II. Title.
III. Series: Highsmith, Carol M., 1946–   Pictorial souvenir.
F309.3.H55   1998
917.5904´63—dc21   97-40005
                                              CIP

8   7   6   5   4   3   2   1

————

Project Editor: Donna Lee Lurker
Production Supervisor: Michael Siebert
Designed by Robert L. Wiser, Archetype Press, Inc., Washington, D.C.

PAGES 2–3: It's easy
to see why Broward
County is called
the "Venice of
Florida." Singer
Barbara Mandrell
lives along one of the
canals that connect
Fort Lauderdale with
its spectacular beach.

FOREWORD

Florida, with its tropical enclaves of bobbing boats, exotic birds, pristine beaches, and golf courses, is America's vision of paradise. In summer, the climate in some South Florida communities is often cooler than New York. In winter, most of the state never sees sleet or snow. Florida seemingly has something for everyone. Nature lovers marvel at the breathtaking flowers, from orchids to blazing stars to flowering water hyacinths, that thrive in Florida's hammocks and marshes, or the Everglades—the incredible, slow-moving, fifty-mile-wide "River of Grass," whose sweet water runs only six inches to three feet deep in most locations.

The state is also the home of gigantic theme parks, seaquariums and serpentariums, jungle and bird gardens, battlefield sites, Indian mounds, and other eccentric man-made attractions, that have made it America's playground. Even as early as the sixteenth century, Florida was identified as a place to relax and enjoy the outdoors: French painter Jacques Le Moyne de Morgues depicted the Timucua Indians swimming, boating, fishing, and frolicking in this natural fairyland. Florida is home to ten national parks, fifty state parks, three national forests, four state forests, and forty-three-hundred square miles of interior lakes and waterways.

The Sunshine State is naturally the mecca for sports fishermen—more than seven hundred species have been caught in the state's waters—hunters, water-skiers, jet-skiers, windsurfers, divers, hikers, skydivers, and even sponge divers. No other state has all of these: pro and college football, basketball, and baseball; major-league hockey; horse and dog racing; championship tennis, golf, and auto racing; pro rodeos; and even polo. Jai-alai, the fifteenth-century Basque game, is played and wagered on in arenas.

But Florida cannot be stereotyped. One can travel from vast cattle ranches, citrus orchards, truck farms, cotton fields, and wide expanses of saw palmettos, to the lively street cafes on Fort Lauderdale's Las Olas Boulevard, to the swanky and stylish shops on Palm Beach's Worth Avenue, or the world-class museums of art in Sarasota, DeLand, Gainesville, Miami, and Jacksonville. Key West—a 110-mile-long necklace of islands tied by forty-five bridges to the mainland—has been the home of wealthy and famous homeowners, including President Harry S Truman, novelist Ernest Hemingway, and playwright Tennessee Williams. Miami Beach, with its array of small Art Deco hotels and gigantic apartment buildings and resort hotels, has become a familiar South Florida landmark, and the home of many of America's rich and prominent celebrities.

Florida is one of America's fastest growing and progressive states. It is a go-go place, growing by seven hundred to one thousand people a day. Space missions are launched here, and some of the world's biggest international corporations and banks are headquartered here. Yet, even with all its urban and cultural development, the Sunshine State is still wild and forbidding. In Florida's considerable wilderness—the Okefenokee Swamp in the far north, the Everglades, and mangrove swamps of the far south—alligators, crocodiles, four kinds of poisonous snakes, and plants whose sap can kill are not tourist attractions to be trifled with.

Sunny. Lush. Aqua. Orange. Neon. Balmy. Sweet. Ancient. Ultramodern. Multicultural. Florida offers a kaleidoscope of sights and experiences not soon forgotten.

OVERLEAF: One can almost feel Miami's vibrancy in its shimmering nighttime skyline. Yet it was barely a century ago that Henry Flagler carved a settlement out of a dense subtropical wilderness. "Boomtown U.S.A." in the 1920s, this polyglot international business capital exploded again in the 1990s with new skyscrapers, sports teams, and restaurants.

Nobel Prize-winning author Ernest Hemingway wrote eight of his most famous novels, notably A Farewell to Arms *and* For Whom the Bell Tolls, *at his Spanish Colonial-style home in Key West (right). Hemingway kept nearly fifty cats—including several six-toed varieties—on the grounds, and some of their direct descendants still loll about. Also on the key, in the courtyard of a Civil War fort called West Martello Tower, are the lush plantings of the Key West Garden Club (opposite)— one of the island's last free tourist attractions. The fort, which was captured by federal troops, is highlighted by vaulted ceilings, gun mounts, and a conservatory. The botanical gardens feature rare native, exotic, and tropical specimens, an exhaustive catalogue of which is available at the door.*

8

Key West's old Strand Theater (opposite) is now the home of Ripley's Believe It or Not "odditorium." Sloppy Joe's Bar (top left), where the sandwich of the same name is said to have originated, was Ernest Hemingway's favorite watering hole. It changed locations in 1933 after the landlord raised the rent from $3.75 to more than $5 a month. The proprietors now spend hundreds of times that much each month. President Truman kept a winter retreat at the "Little White House" (bottom left) on the grounds of a military barracks in Key West's Old Town. The neighborhood has been developed into an eclectic mix of condominiums and family homes.

In 1982, Jim and Frankie Hendricks bought the African Queen (above)—the boat featured in the classic 1951 Humphrey Bogart-Katherine Hepburn movie. They moved it to Key Largo harbor, where they own a Holiday Inn. The boat, built in 1912 in England, served as an actual African steamer. The Hendrickses found it blistering in a cow pasture near Ocala, Florida. Sunset's many hues at the Marathon Marina (right) delight strollers on Marathon Key. The Everglades' slowly moving "River of Grass" (overleaf), more than one hundred miles wide, eventually drains into Florida Bay. There are scattered dry spots, called "hammocks," on which deer, bears, and an occasional cougar can be spotted.

Alligators are not to be trifled with in the Everglades (left), where they abound. The gator uses camouflage—its remarkable resemblance to a floating log—to glide close to unsuspecting prey. Small game—and even an occasional deer, cow, or human— will wander too close to the water's edge and be pounced upon by the beasts, who look ponderous but can rush out of the water with remarkable quickness. The thrashing alligator will then twist and drown its terrified victims. Once an officially endangered species, the gators have made such a comeback that they are straying into residential canals and yards. Few Florida palm trees are harvested in the wild. They are carefully cultivated in irrigated fields like the High Hopes Nursery's spread (above) south of Miami.

17

Hundreds of parrots (above), cockateels, and other chattery, brightly plumed mimics star in four daily shows at Parrot Jungle and Gardens, southwest of Miami. Visitors can also get a close-up view of reptiles, small mammals, birds of prey, and more than twelve hundred varieties of exotic plants. There's a flamingo preserve there—and also at the Miami Metrozoo (left). In South Miami, too, the spectacular Vizcaya Gardens (overleaf) were a playground in the sun on the grounds of the winter retreat of James Deering, co-founder of the International Harvester Company. The gardens and majestic Italianate mansion at the edge of Biscayne Bay are now a museum.

Little Havana (right), along Calle Ocho— Eighth Street—is a colorful neighborhood of markets, shops, and parks. Two waves of Cuban immigrants settled in the Miami district, where there are now statues to heroes of Cuban independence, a "sidewalk of stars" similar to Hollywood's Walk of Fame, innumerable Spanish signs, and restaurants serving delicacies like fried Cuban sandwiches. CocoWalk (above) is a collage of stylish fashion and food establishments in the heart of Miami's oldest neighborhood— Coconut Grove. By the time Miami became a city in 1896, Cocoanut Grove, settled by Bahamian immigrants, was already thriving. In 1919 it dropped the "a" from its name.

Because more than five hundred thousand Cuban refugees registered at a processing center in Miami's first skyscraper (above) in the 1960s, the structure became known as "Freedom Tower." The 1924 landmark, which housed the offices of the Miami News, was extensively renovated in the mid-1990s. The view from the top floors of the First Union Bank Building (right), overlooking the Miami River, is nothing short of spectacular. There are more skyscrapers across the river in the Brickell area of downtown. Although Miami's gleaming skyscrapers give a first impression of another sterile glass-and-steel urban canyon, the city below is alive with activity—in dozens of languages. Miami is the undisputed financial and trading gateway to all the Americas, but its banks, malls, and commercial-district shops represent cultures—and cater to customers—from around the world.

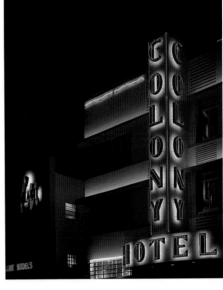

Miami's Metromover light-rail system (opposite) has two overhead loops through downtown and extensions north and south across the city. The China Grill (left) and the Colony Hotel (above) are glowing proof that, at night, Miami Beach's South Beach is a sea of neon. The 1935 Colony Hotel, on Ocean Avenue, falls within the city's historic district, so the building's illumination must respect the original design, when neon was more of an accent than a prominent feature. The newer round restaurant and office tower stands outside the district, so, like a Times Square or Las Vegas building, it is free to spiral its neon up the entire building.

South Beach (opposite and above) has one of the world's largest concentrations of Art Deco buildings, which make a fascinating architectural statement, daytime or at night and with or without neon accent. The Art Deco name derives from the 1925 Exposition International des Arts Decoratifs et Industriels Modernes in Paris, which introduced novel combinations of Pre-Columbian, Cubist, "machine Expressionist," and even "Zig Zag Moderne" styles. Sharp corners, sparse fixtures, electric embellishments, and pastel shades were some of the features admired and emulated by the captains of commerce who developed Miami Beach. Northward from South Beach (overleaf), Miami Beach is lined with condominiums, modern hotel towers, and rental apartments. With the development of even swankier resort communities farther up the Florida Coast, Miami Beach suffered a precipitous decline. Extensively renovated, it has since bounced back to again become a favorite haunt of the world's "beautiful people."

Fort Lauderdale (opposite) is a shining Florida success story. Long a scruffy collegiate "Spring Break" destination, the city has revitalized its world-class beach with a wave-shaped promenade wall and walkway, trimmed with tempting cafés. A spectacular performing-arts center capped its cultural renaissance. Up the coast in Palm Beach, Worth Avenue (left) remains one of America's poshest shopping destinations. The Boca Raton Resort & Club (above), founded as the Cloister Inn in 1926, typifies the elegance of that seaside resort. Its "Boca pink," now a recognized color, is designed to represent the "perfect sunset." The Breakers (overleaf) in Palm Beach has also been one of the "Gold Coast's" favorite wintertime addresses of socialites and celebrities.

Previous pages: America's oldest city gate, not unexpectedly, can be seen in the nation's oldest city— Saint Augustine— founded in 1565. The gate was part of the defensive wall that protected the city from attack. It, and much of the restored area to which it opens, is now maintained by the National Park Service. Saint Augustine is a history-lover's paradise. Inside the oldest surviving Spanish colonial structure, the Gonzáles-Alvarez House (above) is a museum whose exhibits cover the more than four centuries of history of the old colonial outpost. The site has been continuously occupied by Europeans or Americans since the early 1600s. Restored historic buildings— including America's oldest wooden schoolhouse in the foreground—front Saint George Street (right) along the old Spanish Quarter. The cedar and cypress school building was constructed during the second Spanish period, from 1784 to 1821. Railroad baron Henry Flagler built more than fifteen magnificent structures in America's "Southern Newport," including Baptist, Methodist, and Presbyterian churches. His crowning achievement was the Ponce de León Hotel (overleaf), now owned by Flagler College.

Bustling Jacksonville (left), on Florida's northeast "First Coast," is known for its festive, and mostly free, festivals, including those for kite, powerboating, pier-fishing, and sand-castle-building enthusiasts. The Mug Race sailboat regatta on the Saint Johns River is, at forty-two miles, the longest in the world. Jacksonville became a major-league sports city with the arrival of a National Football League team in 1995.

A likeness of its Jaguar mascot (above) menaces outside Memorial Stadium. Idyllic dunes (overleaf) dot remote reaches that share Amelia Island with fabulous resorts, elegant hotels, and Fernandina Beach—the historic border port between Spanish Florida and English or American territory. Eight flags—including those of pirates, French Huguenots, and the southern Confederacy—have flown over the island.

Florida confronts its
sometimes-racist
history forthrightly.
The stories of both
dreadful and positive
episodes in the state's
African-American
history—from Ku
Klux Klan atrocities
and demeaning
products and minstrel
shows, to achieve-
ments by war heroes
and statesmen—
are recounted at the
state's Black Archives
(above) in Tallahas-
see's old Freedman's

(later Union) Bank.
For example, U.S.
Supreme Court
Justice Thurgood
Marshall's life's story
is told in detail at the
archive. Many of the
city's pioneers, their
slaves, and white
and black Civil War
troops from both
sides—Tallahassee
was the only
southern capital
never captured by
Union forces—are
buried in Old City
Cemetery (right).

Florida's state govern-
ment is quartered in
a nondescript office
tower. The adjacent
Old State Capitol
(opposite), built in
1845, has been restored
to its 1902 appearance,
with red candy-striped
awnings, stained-glass
dome, and classic
rotunda. When there
was talk of demolish-
ing the landmark in
the 1970s, opponents
successfully fought the
measure; the building
is now a museum of
Florida's political
history. A walk around
the lake in the
Panhandle town of
DeFuniak Springs is a
stroll into Victoriana,
when grand homes
incorporated elaborate
architectural details.
Pictured (above) are
painstakingly restored
houses on Circle
Drive. DeFuniak
Springs was a winter
headquarters of the
New York Chau-
tauqua movement.
From 1885 to 1922,
thousands of visitors
traveled there for
"instruction, recre-
ation, amusement, fel-
lowship, elocution,
philosophy, and
cookery." DeFuniak's
Chautauqua is still
celebrated, beginning
with Illumination
Night in February and
continuing through
a Chautauqua
Festival in April.

Tampa (right) is
Florida's third-largest
city, behind Miami
and Jacksonville, but
it is the second-largest
employment center.
Its port is the nation's
eleventh-largest in
cargo tonnage (first
in Florida), and its
airport is consistently
rated tops in America
by the Airline Passen-
gers Association.
The dock in the fore-
ground accommodates
water taxis that ply
the Hillsborough
River. Like Henry
Flagler on Florida's
east coast, Henry
Plant built the
railroad that opened
the west coast to
development. Plant,
too, erected luxurious
hotels to accommo-
date wealthy "snow-
birds." His jewel was
the onion-domed,
five-hundred-room
Tampa Bay Hotel in
Tampa (opposite),
built in 1891. The
strange architectural
concoction—mixing
Victorian, Spanish,
and Moorish
elements, is now the
main building of the
University of Tampa.

Ybor City is historic cigarmaking district. But today, with its lively clubs, galleries, and brewpub, it's more like the SoHo of the South. On Ybor's Seventh Avenue is the hand-tiled façade of the Columbia Restaurant (opposite). The intricate decoration stretches around the block. Carmela Varsalona (above) began wrapping cigars in factories as a sixteen-year-old. In her prime, she could produce four hundred hand-rolled cigars a day. The process involves rolling a rough bunch of filler leaves, then squeezing them into a press to obtain the cigar's distinctive shape. Next, the hand-rolled cigar is wrapped in a select outer leaf and snipped. Ideally, a fine cigar then ages a month or more to reduce the moisture in the tobacco leaves. Mrs. Varsalona now helps her grandson, Jim Tyre, roll cigars for his Cammorata cigar shop in Tampa's Urban Center.

PREVIOUS PAGES:
In 1905, in Saint Petersburg, George Turner purchased a home along a dirt road north of town and discovered a large sinkhole and a shallow lake on the property. An avid horticulturist, Turner lined the lake with drainage tile, then turned it and the sinkhole into habitats for exotic plants. Visits to his gardens became a Suncoast tradition for which the enterprising Turner charged a nickel. Today Sunken Gardens is Florida's oldest family-owned attraction. John Ringling, the youngest of seven Ringling Brothers, and his wife, Mable, settled in Sarasota, where the brothers' circus wintered. Ringling collected art on a grand scale and built a museum next to his home in which to display it. In the courtyard (opposite), are beautiful columns, fountains, and statues, including a bronze cast of Michelangelo's David (right), the only one in the western world.

PREVIOUS PAGES: The area of Central Florida around Kissimmee and Saint Cloud is world-renowned orange country. Palm trees are a classic Florida symbol, and in Orlando, the palms outside the Peabody Hotel sparkle at night (opposite) year-round. Orlando's Universal Studios Florida (above) is a working motion-picture and television studio and theme park. Its characters, including Frankenstein, Woody Woodpecker, Rocky and Bullwinkle, Yogi Bear and Scooby Doo, and E. T. derive from Universal's film and television characters. So do its rides— including "Back to the Future" and "Earthquake"—and its live shows, taken from The Wild, Wild West; The Blues Brothers; Terminator 2; and other Universal productions. The theme park's most famous ride brings visitors into close contact with a thirty-two-foot, three-ton, animated "Jaws" great white shark. Wandering the sets are celebrity look-alikes modeled on W. C. Fields, the Marx Brothers, Popeye, Mae West, Stan Laurel and Oliver Hardy, Charlie Chaplin, and others.

At Sea World of Florida, Virgil Pelican (opposite) delights children and amateur photographers with his flapping dances and other antics. Shamu the Whale is the park's big draw, but playful dolphins (above) entertain visitors as well. These bottlenose dolphins, which humans came to adore through the Flipper movies and Jacques Cousteau's epic underwater photography, chatter among themselves. The sound is picked up by underwater microphones and broadcast to Sea World visitors. The sounds serve as communication, but the mammals also read the echo from each other's calls to help locate objects in the water. Like whales, dolphins have blowholes, out of which they spew excess water when they surface to take deep breaths. These intelligent creatures will lead fish away from trawlers' nets. In captivity they will jump in formation, blow bubbles, and allow children to nuzzle their foreheads.

Titles available in the Pictorial Souvenir series